SIMPLY
Guitar

hinkler

*This book is dedicated to Ian and Dianne MacKay
(Mum and Dad) for everything they have done for me.*

Published by Hinkler Books Pty Ltd 2013
45–55 Fairchild Street
Heatherton Victoria 3202 Australia
www.hinkler.com.au

hinkler

Design © Hinkler Books Pty Ltd 2013
Text © Steve MacKay 2005

Creative Director: Sam Grimmer
Design: Sam Grimmer & Hinkler Design Studio
Photography: Ned Meldrum
Prepress: Graphic Print Group
Typesetting: MPS Limited

Special thanks to Metropolis Audio.

ISBN: 978 1 7435 2885 3

Printed and bound in China

The Publishers and their respective employees or agents will not accept
responsibility for injury or damage occasioned to any person as a result of
participation in the activities described in this book.

CONTENTS

Introduction. 4
How to Purchase Your First Guitar 6
Know Your Instrument – Acoustic Guitar 8
Know Your Instrument – Electric Guitar. 9
What You Need. 10
Correct Posture 11
How to Learn What and Where the Notes Are 12
Know All the Notes 13
Position Playing and Playing 'In Position' 14
Understanding Common Guitar Diagrams 15
Tuning the Guitar 16
Technique Fundamentals 18
The Caterpillar 20
Basic Major Chords 22
Basic Minor Chords. 23
Basic Chord Progressions 24
Chord to Chord Transition Exercises 25
How Chords Are Built and How to Build Them . . .26
What You Need to Know About the Major Scale. . . . 27
Chord Formulas 28
Test Yourself – 20 Questions 30
Putting the Groove Into Your Strumming. 32
Reading the Chord Progressions with Counting . . .33
Barre Chords. 34
How to Play Barre Chords 35
How to Use Barre Chords 36
Moving On 38
Finger Style Playing 39
Finger Style Patterns 40
Advanced Chords 43
Chord Finder 47
A. 48
B. 50
C. 52
D. 54
E. 56
F. 58
G. 60
Frequently Asked Questions 62
Conclusion 63
About the Author 64

INTRODUCTION

This book has been written for those of you who may have never played guitar and feel a little intimidated by it, and those of you who already play, but need some of the gaps in your knowledge and technique bridged before you can progress any further.

I have taught students of all ages and skill levels and I find the same recurring questions keep coming up:
'It seems like there is at least a million notes on the guitar ... How am I supposed to learn and remember them? How do I get my fingers to do what I tell them to do? What do all these fancy terminologies mean? What is that chord and how do I play it? Why don't the songs I'm trying to play sound like they should? Why does my guitar sound like a box with elastic bands on it?'

The first thing we have to get straight before we begin is that playing guitar is not a walk in the park. It takes hard work, dedication to practice and a love of music to get any results. Reading this book and following the DVD should open a few doors, but it is up to you to walk through them.

Like learning almost anything new, it can be as difficult or as simple as you want it to be, or as difficult or as simple as the teacher makes it. If you currently have a guitar teacher and you feel learning guitar is an impossible feat, either ask for the explanations to be simplified or get a new guitar teacher!

After reading this book and watching the DVD you should:

• Understand the ins and outs and dos and don'ts of guitar.

• Know the names of the strings.

• Know how to find all the notes on the guitar.

• Know what chords are and how to play them.

• Know how chords are formed.

• Know how to read and write tablature.

• Be able to play through chord progressions with relative ease.

Above all, I hope you would have gained a deeper understanding of what guitar is, how you can move forward with it as a creative and expressive tool and, most importantly, how to have fun with it!

HOW TO PURCHASE YOUR FIRST GUITAR

There are a lot of misconceptions about buying a guitar. People tend to bypass the less aesthetically pleasing or second-hand guitars for the cheaper, shiny-looking brand new ones that come with the free leopard-skin strap. As hard as it is to understand, the cool looking guitars aren't always the best to play. So how do you know what is good and what is unsuitable?

After years of buying the wrong guitars and learning the hard way, I've found there are two golden rules:

1 Spend as much money as your budget will allow. You get what you pay for.

2 Whenever you buy a guitar, you must have it SET UP! Then from that point on, have it set up at least once a year. I cannot stress the importance of this enough. When you buy a car, you don't drive it until it falls apart – you have it serviced. Guitars are the same.

So what is a set-up and where do I get one?
With the right expert (expert being the operative word), a set-up can turn what seems like a hopeless piece of firewood into a nice playable guitar. You wouldn't go to a butcher to get your appendix out, so make sure you don't take your guitar to Bob over the back fence who has a new screwdriver set. Make some enquiries in music stores and, even better, ask any working guitarist. The aim is to go with the most reputable person you can.

When you're in the store, what should you look for?
Does it feel good to hold?
Sit down on a chair (preferably with no arms) and hold the guitar as you would if you were going to play it. If you are holding it correctly, it should mould to your body and you shouldn't feel any discomfort.

What is the action like?
The 'action' is the distance between the strings and the fret board. Ideally, a nice low action is the best for a number of reasons, the main reason being it makes playing guitar easier!

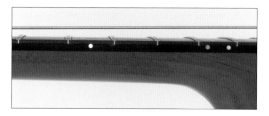

High Action: The distance between the strings and the fret board is quite substantial. This makes it uncomfortable and difficult to press the fingers down on notes. WARNING: High action will impair your ability to progress on the guitar if not fixed with a set-up!

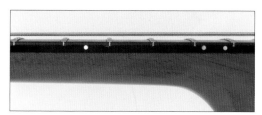

Low Action: The distance between the strings and the fret board is slight but they do not actually touch. This makes pressing the fingers down on notes more comfortable and easier. WARNING: If the action is too low, the strings will buzz on the frets and affect the sound of the guitar. A good way to tell if this is happening is to play every single note on the guitar with one finger. If it sounds nice and clean, there's no

problem. If there are strange buzzes and inconsistencies in the sound, the action is set too low. This can also be remedied by a good set-up.

Does it stay in tune?
Playing an out-of-tune guitar is like eating your breakfast cereal with bat milk. I've never done it, but I'm sure it doesn't taste right! Make sure the guitar is tuned before you test it, and then when it is tuned, play it solidly for around 5 minutes. If it stays in tune, great. If it is out of tune, it could be fixed with a set-up, but if you can't find a guitar that stays in tune after 5 minutes of playing, I'd probably go to another guitar store! If you can't play yet, ask the person selling it to tune it and then demonstrate the guitar for you – no stairway to heaven!

KNOW YOUR INSTRUMENT

It is imperative to study the following two pages so that you know your instrument. Understanding what part or component of the guitar is being referred to when you read this book, watch the DVD or invest in any other instructional information is a big advantage and will avoid confusion about terminology.

ACOUSTIC GUITAR

headstock

machine heads

nut

neck

frets

body

sound hole

bridge

ELECTRIC GUITAR

headstock

machine heads

nut

neck

frets

body

pickup

volume/tone controls

bridge

pickup selector

WHAT YOU NEED

It would be great for the development of your playing and practice to try to purchase the following items, which are available from any good music store. Don't be afraid to ask for a demonstration!

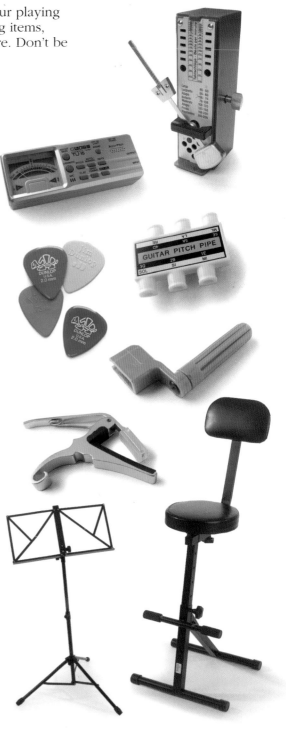

Metronome
Metronomes keep time for you, either by beeping or ticking to a tempo (speed) and time signature (amount of beats) that you set manually.

Electronic guitar tuner
Tuners make tuning the guitar an easy task. They have a simple needle or light that indicates when the string is in tune.

Pitch pipe
A great little tool if you are tuning your guitar by ear. Using a pitch pipe will give you a reference pitch to tune one string. You then tune the remaining strings from the string tuned to the reference pitch.

Assortment of plectrums
Plectrums are those little things you see people strumming and picking the guitar with. Plectrums (or picks) come in all shapes and sizes. I recommend Jim Dunlop Jazz III picks or anything above 1mm thick (for a softer sound experiment with softer picks).

String winder
A nifty device created to speed up the process of winding on new strings.

Capo
A capo is a clamp that you place across all six strings to alter the pitch of the guitar.

Good stool or armless chair
It seems simple, but if you're going to be playing guitar a lot, make sure you have a comfortable chair or stool with no arms, as arms can get in the way of holding the instrument correctly or can damage the guitar.

Music stand
A music stand is great because it enables you to shorten the distance between what you're reading and your left hand (right hand if you are left handed).

CORRECT POSTURE

It is possible to get back, neck, arm, hand and finger injuries from holding the guitar with incorrect posture. The most important thing to remember is that you should never be tense or in pain – always remember to relax!

   Notice how the guitar shape is usually designed with the human body in mind. The curvature of the guitar body allows the guitar to sit comfortably on your thigh, and the neck is scaled so that your left arm (right arm if you are left handed) is free to move up and down the guitar with ease.

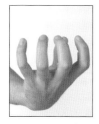

How your left hand should be positioned
(right if you are left handed)

Have your thumb centred on the back of the guitar neck and relatively straight (back view). Your fingers should be curved and straight. This creates what is commonly referred to as 'the claw' grip, with the second and third fingers touching the thumb (the claw). We will cover specifics later in the book, but in the meantime try and emulate these pictures to the best of your ability.

Holding a plectrum (pick)

The first three step-by-step pictures demonstrate how to hold the plectrum. The fourth picture is simply a different view of the third picture, taken from underneath the hand as opposed to above it.

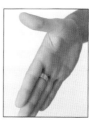

1. Put your hand out as if you are going to do a karate chop
2. Bend your index finger inward as far as it will go comfortably
3. Sit the plectrum in between the outside of your index finger and your thumb

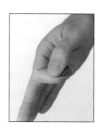

The plectrum should look as though it is coming out of the side of your thumb. The remaining fingers should be outstretched and relaxed. The pressure you apply to the plectrum should be minimal – try not to tense up when you play!

HOW TO LEARN WHAT AND WHERE THE NOTES ARE

First things first – what are the names of the strings? There is a lot of 'stuff' to remember when you start learning a new instrument. I find the best way to commit seemingly random ideas to memory is to create some sort of connection between what you are learning with something you already know, or that you could easily memorise. The best way to do this is by remembering by association. For example, the names of the strings on the guitar (from the thinnest to thickest) are E, B, G, D, A and E. There is no pattern or logic to the order, so make an acronym:

E Easter
B Bunny
G Goes
D Dancing
A At
E Easter

How many notes are there in the musical alphabet?

There are 7 NATURAL notes in Western music! They are: **A B C D E F G**

You may have noticed that the musical alphabet is identical to the normal alphabet, only it stops at G. Keep in mind, these are not all the notes in music. There are also sharps (that look like this – #) and flats (that look like this – b). What follows is an explanation to give you an understanding of how sharps and flats relate to natural notes:

Ab (flat)   **A** (natural)   **A#** (sharp)

Ab is one fret back from A natural.
A# is one fret forward from A natural.

This may come as a surprise for the less musically-inclined folks reading this but in total, there are only 12 notes in Western music! Here they are:

A   Bb/A#   B   C   Db/C#   D

Eb/D#   E   F   Gb/F#   G   Ab/G#

Notice how Bb (for example) can also be called A#. Whether you use sharps or flats is dictated by what key the music you are playing is in. This is a topic you don't have to worry about just yet.

It is extremely helpful if you can memorise the musical alphabet. To make things easier, you don't have to memorise the flats. We will only deal with the sharps for the time being. Referring back to what I said about turning things into acronyms or sayings earlier, the easiest way to memorise the musical alphabet is to identify what is different from the regular alphabet pattern we all know.

Here are a couple of suggested ways to remember this:

• Every note has a sharp after it except "BE"

• There is no B# and no E#

Run through this until you know it as well as you know your own name (it'll come in handy very soon!).

KNOW ALL
THE NOTES

Neck perspective

There are many different ways of looking at the guitar when you play. You can look at the neck in chunks, diagonally, up and down, randomly and countless other ways. I suggest looking at it by the neck, string by string and horizontally, starting from the 1st fret all the way up to the 12th fret, almost like you have 6 keyboards lined up in front of you.

Now is a good time to mention the importance of reviewing everything slowly and carefully to ensure you have a good grasp on what is being taught.

Learning all the notes

Now that you have the right perspective and can look at the neck in a simple way, all you need to do is apply everything you have learnt so far (string names and musical alphabet) and develop your ability to navigate around the neck.

1. Play an OPEN A string (open means no fingers pressing down on the fret board).
2. Now put your first finger on the first fret. That note is A#.

3. Move up one more fret. That note is B.
4. Move up one more fret. That note is C.

Recognise the pattern?

A	A#	B	C	C#	D	D#	E	F

F#	G	G#

This same technique can be applied to all of the strings. Say you start on the OPEN D string. Now put your first finger on the first fret. That note is D#. Move up one more fret. That note is E, and so on.

A	A#	B	C	C#	D	D#	E	F

F#	G	G#

Now that you know the names of the strings, the musical alphabet and how to join the two together and navigate your way around the neck, all you have to do is become quicker and more proficient at doing so. The more you do something, the less you need to consciously think about it. Eventually you will be able to look at the neck and just see the notes.

Tip:
Memorise the notes that fall on the dots. By doing this, you have more points of reference to figure out other unknown notes using the musical alphabet.

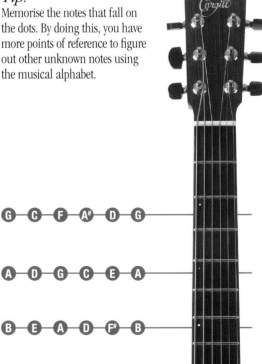

Position Playing and Playing 'In Position'

Position playing is quite a simple concept that is designed to help the student understand the correct fingering of any particular music, be it a song, scale or chord.

If I were to be in 1st position, it would mean:

1st finger is on the 1st fret, 2nd finger is on the 2nd fret, 3rd finger is on the 3rd fret, 4th finger is on the 4th fret

If I were to be in 5th position it would mean:

1st finger is on the 5th fret, 2nd finger is on the 6th fret, 3rd finger is on the 7th fret, 4th finger is on the 8th fret

If this fret was the 9th fret, and your fingers were lined up exactly like this only starting from the 9th fret onwards, you would be in '9th position', and so on.

When in position, generally speaking, no finger should move from its designated fret. There are a number of reasons why you would want to implement position guidelines:

- To make playing the song easier and more fluent.
- Correct technique (traditionally there is a right and a wrong technique and bad habits are hard to break!).
- You have more than one finger so use them!

UNDERSTANDING COMMON GUITAR DIAGRAMS

There are two main types of diagrams that you will encounter when playing the guitar.

Chord diagrams

These are pictures of the guitar neck with relevant information about which fret and what fingers to use. (A chord is more than one note played together at the same time – usually a minimum of three notes.)

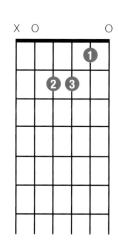

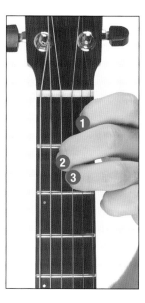

- Chord diagrams are upright pictures of the guitar neck.

- The numbers represent which fingers you should use.

- The 'X' means don't play this string. The 'O' means play the string open.

Tablature

This is a visual guide showing where to put your fingers.

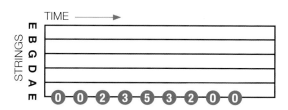

- Tablature is the easiest way to communicate music notation on the guitar.

- The lines represent the strings.

- The numbers represent the fret numbers you press on with your fingers.

- Sometimes a second set of smaller numbers is written underneath the fret numbers. These numbers would tell you which finger to use.

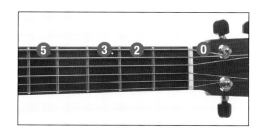

TUNING THE GUITAR

The two most common ways to tune a guitar are:

1. Using a digital guitar tuner
2. By ear

The harsh reality about tuning a guitar by ear is that some people are tone deaf and can't tell if something is in tune or not. You do need an ear for music to know if the notes that you are playing together are in tune. In saying that, nobody usually starts tuning perfectly straight away. It takes practice, like anything else does.

The first thing you need to do when you are tuning your guitar by ear is to either assume the first string is relatively in tune, and tune the other strings from that, or tune the strings to the corresponding reference pitch from a keyboard or pitch pipe.

Tuning the guitar, assuming
the first string is in tune

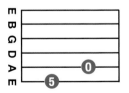

Play these two notes
after each other

Because you have assumed the first string is in tune, you will only have to adjust the tuning key for the second string, matching what you hear from the reference pitch on the first string.
  Is what you hear higher (sharper) or lower (flatter) to our reference pitch on the first string? Hopefully your guitar is strung properly, so that if you turn the tuning key for the second string anti-clockwise, the pitch will get higher, and if you turn the tuning key clockwise, the pitch will get lower.

NOTE: To know if your guitar has been strung properly refer to this picture. All your strings should wrap around the machine heads from the inside out, like so.

- From this point, you need to ascertain whether the second string sounds higher or lower compared to your reference pitch on the first string, then turn the tuning key clockwise or anti-clockwise accordingly.

- The notes should sound identical.

- When a string is out of tune you can usually hear a 'wow-wow' type of effect when you play it against your reference pitch.

OUT OF TUNE

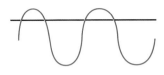

reference pitch

pitch of string
to be tuned

IN TUNE

reference pitch

pitch of
tuned string

When you feel you have the second string sounding identical to the reference pitch on the first string, the second string now becomes the reference pitch for the third string, and so on and so on.

To make sure you are getting the hang of this, let's go through tuning the third string to the reference pitch on the second string.

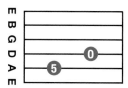

Play these two notes after each other

Is what you hear higher (sharper) or lower (flatter) than our reference pitch on the second string?

• From this point, you need to ascertain whether the second string sounds higher or lower compared to your reference pitch on the first string, then turn the tuning key clockwise or anti-clockwise accordingly.

• The notes should sound identical.

• When a string is out of tune you can usually hear a 'wow-wow' type of effect when you play it against your reference pitch.

Here are all the reference pitch notes for tuning the whole guitar in this fashion.

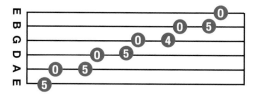

NOTE: This section on tuning can be very confusing, so don't worry if you don't quite get it when you read it. After watching the DVD and reading the section, you will really have a better understanding of how tuning works.

TECHNIQUE FUNDAMENTALS

I think one of the most important attributes a student of guitar can have is the ability to identify where they are going wrong with their technique, in order to put into practice what to do right. Here are a few basic 'rules' to follow.

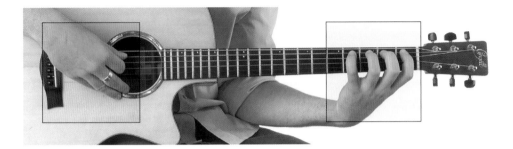

RIGHT HAND RULES (pick technique)

- Fingers anchored to the body of the guitar
- Correct grip on the pick
- Alternate picking (down, up, down, up)

LEFT HAND RULES

- Tips of fingers
- Fingers middle of the frets
- Curved fingers
- Straight claw-like hand shape
- Position playing
- Thumb in the middle of the neck

Now that you know what you are supposed to do, you really have to implement it in your playing with zero tolerance for deviation. In other words, no matter what you are playing, even if it is 'Mary Had A Little Lamb', aim to get every note played perfectly and aim to get your technique as flawless as you possibly can. Teaching yourself this way of practice will eventually lead you to do it naturally, and you will progress ten times faster than someone who practises without taking notice of what they are actually doing.

Alternate picking

This part is very important to those of you out there who want to be able to play guitar at light speed (and shred like an 80's metal god!). For everyone else, it is important to learn the correct picking technique in order to play notes and chords with more ease. This is a hard lesson to learn if you have already been playing with a plectrum and haven't been alternate picking.

The idea is quite simple – when you pick down, pick up afterwards, regardless of whether you are changing strings or staying on the one string. The reason for doing so is to save time and make things easy on yourself. 'What goes down, must come up!'

Picking down   Picking up

Tap your foot! When ever you play guitar, tap your foot! It is as important as anything written on this page!

THE CATERPILLAR

For a beginner, this exercise can be the guitar equivalent of a headache, a hangover and endless re-runs of your worst nightmare! No, it's not that bad really. Just remember, no pain, no gain! The great thing I have found about the ol' 'Caterpillar' is that if it is practised daily and with the technique fundamentals outlined on the previous page, it can really accelerate your playing ability substantially.

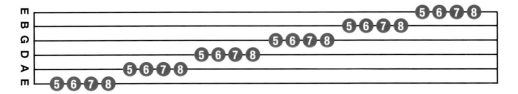

As you can see by the tablature above, it looks quite simple, but here's the trick:

1. Play each note without removing any of your fingers until they are needed to play another note.

2. Keep all of your fingers down so that you only move one finger at a time.

3. If you hear a buzz, or an inconsistency in the sound, or forget to implement the rules outlined on page 18, START OVER!

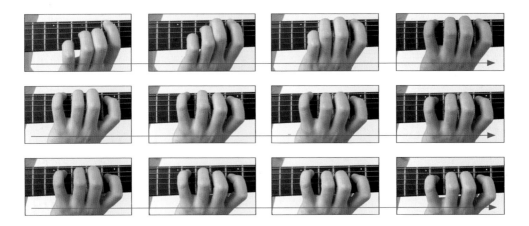

Repeat those two steps over and over until you can play through this exercise ten times at a slow pace without any mistakes. Do this religiously at least two minutes a day, then gradually increase the pace at a rate you can handle.

Now apply the same method to the next three strings, and remember, if you make a mistake, slow down and start from the beginning until you find a speed that enables you to run through the Caterpillar perfectly.

Basic Chords

These two pages cover all the basic major and minor chord shapes in alphabetical order. You will notice some chords are missing because they are more complicated and harder to play (we will get to those later in the book).

Basic Major Chords

A major

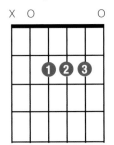

C major

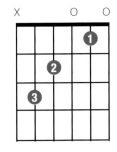

D major

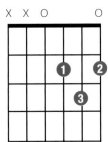

E major

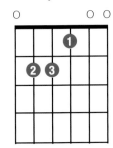

G major

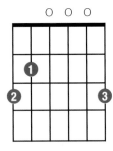

Major chords are happy sounding chords

Go through and play each chord from this page and the previous page, one after the other, saying the name of the chord out loud as you play it. It is very important that you know what you are playing, and by reinforcing the chord names verbally to yourself you can more easily commit them to memory.

BASIC MINOR CHORDS

A minor

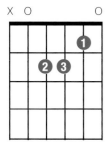 

D minor

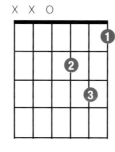 

E minor

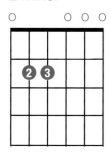 

Minor chords are sad sounding chords

BASIC CHORD PROGRESSIONS

Now that you have learnt the basic chords and memorised their shapes and names, it's time to put them into practice. Chord progressions are basically chords put into an order that works sonically, like a song!

  You can experiment with strumming these chords any way you like at this stage. The aim is just to get the hang of playing through each chord to the next; we will cover strumming concepts a little later in the book. Run through each of these chord progressions, saying each chord's name as you play it.

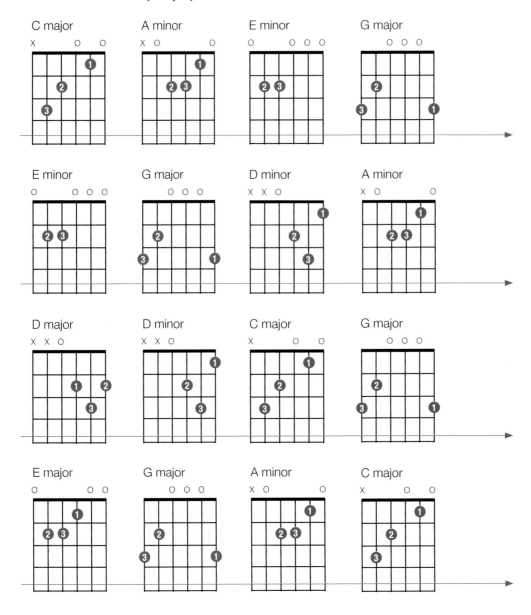

CHORD TO CHORD TRANSITION EXERCISES

Now that you have learnt the basic major and minor chords and played through a few progressions, it's time to make things smoother and easier. The secret to changing chords seamlessly and comfortably is training your fingers to move from chord to chord with minimal movement and visualising the transition.

Most people who learn chords and then start playing through progressions (songs) often play one chord, then completely remove all their fingers to form the next chord, so you end up hearing a chord then a gap while the next chord is being put into place.

I'm sure you could probably relate to what I am saying after your first attempt at playing through a chord progression fluently. It's harder than it looks, right?

So to get you heading in the right direction, let's break down the first chord progression on the previous page step by step (watch the DVD for a demonstration about putting this theory into practice).

Let's start with the C major chord to the A minor chord.

- Lift ONLY your third finger from the 3rd fret, A string
- Place it on the 2nd fret, G string without moving any other fingers
- Now you are playing A minor

Now the A minor chord to the E minor chord.

- Lift your first finger from the 1st fret, B string
- Prepare to place it on the 2nd fret, A string
- At the same time, remove your third finger from the 2nd fret, G string altogether

- Now implement the above instructions in one 'pivoting' movement
- You are now playing the E minor chord

Now the E minor chord to the G major chord.

- Lift your second finger from the 2nd fret, D string
- Prepare to place it on the 3rd fret, low E string
- At the same time, prepare to place your fourth finger on the 3rd fret, high E string and your third finger on the 3rd fret, B string
- Now implement the above instructions in one 'pivoting' movement
- You are now playing the G major chord

It sounds a little more complicated to read than it does to watch, so make sure you follow up this page by watching the corresponding section on the DVD.

Play through all of the chord progressions on page 24, strumming each chord 4 times – down then up, down then up (change chord), down then up, down then up, and so on.

Practise this strumming technique, implementing the chord transition ideas you have just learnt, until each chord flows smoothly into the next and what you are playing is in time and actually sounds like a song.

We will talk about more in-depth strumming patterns a little later in the book, so make sure you have mastered it!

How Chords Are Built and How to Build Them

The next piece of information could sound a little confusing at first, so try and go over it slowly and repeat it to yourself out loud.

Ok, here we go! All chords are made up from formulas. These formulas are simply combinations of notes from the major scale. Another way of looking at it would be pretending chords are cakes.

I know that sounds weird! So to clarify:

- Major scale = Supermarket (has all of the ingredients)
- Formula = Recipe (a combination of the ingredients)
- Chord = Cake (type of cake determined by what the ingredients are)

So far, you have played all the 'simple chords' (chords that have open strings), but you haven't touched on the major scale or formulas yet. So let's start with the major scale.

G major scale

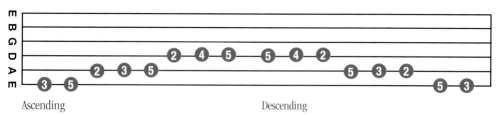

This particular major scale is a G major scale because the starting note is G and it is played in 2nd position.

If I play the exact same shape in 4th position, the starting note will be A and it will be the A major scale.

A major scale

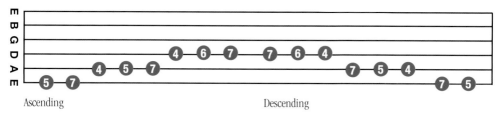

By memorising the 'shape' or the 'pattern' of the scale and moving it to any starting note on the low E string (or A string), you will have that note's major scale. Movable shapes are shapes you can move around!

WHAT YOU NEED TO KNOW ABOUT THE MAJOR SCALE

If you've seen 'The Sound of Music', you've heard the major scale. In fact, it is the most commonly used scale in Western music, and chances are you probably have it solidly embedded in your subconscious from singing nursery rhymes as a kid.

We could go on about the origins and oddities of the major scale but at this point it's safe to say you now know what the major scale is and what chords are, so now we just need cover this 'formula' business.

Formulas are made up of numbers. Those numbers represent notes in the major scale. Now when you play the MAJOR SCALE, number each note 1 to 8 starting from the start like so:

G major scale

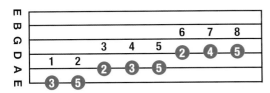

If you play 1 and 8 together you might recognise the shape known as an 'octave'. Octopus, octagon – eight. An octave is the 1st note and the 8th note of the major scale played together.

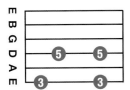

Two fret numbers placed on top of each other means 'play at the same time'.

For the punk rockers, if you play the 1st and the 5th notes together from the major scale, you might recognise the shape known as a 'power chord', or sometimes referred to as a '5th chord' (1st note and 5th note).

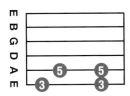

There are working guitarists out there that get away with just playing this one shape but in different positions, so you are almost ready to take on the world!

CHORD FORMULAS

- Every major chord is made up of 1, 3, 5.
  The 1st note, 3rd note and 5th note of the major scale.

- Every minor chord is made up of 1, b3, 5.
  The 1st note, 3rd note flattened and 5th note of the major scale.

AHHHH! What does 3rd note flattened mean?
   I knew you would ask that one – refer back to our musical alphabet on page 12. To 'flatten' a note basically means to take it back one step. So if the 3rd is B, the flattened 3rd will be Bb.

To reinforce the whole formula idea, let's dissect the C major chord. First we need the numbered notes to the C major scale.

Now let's circle the formula 1, 3, 5.

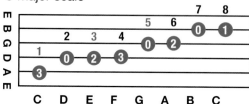

C major scale

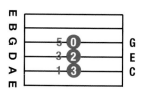

So in order to play a C major chord we need to play the C, E and G notes together somehow. We have four fingers and a thumb to use and six strings. Obviously you cannot play two notes on one string at the same time, so you have to find a way to play those notes together.

Here is the easiest way to play those notes:

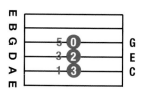

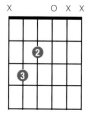

But we still have one finger and three strings left! What happens now? As long as you are playing the correct notes as stipulated in the formula (1st C, 3rd E, 5th G), all you need to do is repeat any of them until you have utilised the strings and the fingers you have left!

Here is the easiest way to do that. Find the choices you have.

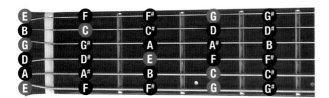

Arrange your fingers and utilise the open strings according to the formula and the choices you have figured out.

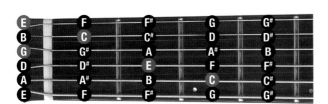
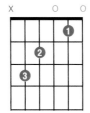

Notice this shape? That's right, it is the good ol' C major chord shape from page 22. Now you know why these chords are called 'basic chord shapes'. Once upon a time somebody figured out that these shapes are the easiest way to represent the formulas needed to construct the major and minor chords!

So hopefully your mind is ticking over with the possibilities. There are only 12 notes in music and 11 different ways to play them on the guitar (six strings, around 22 frets). You have four fingers and a thumb to use and you only need to play the 1st, 3rd and 5th notes of the major scale to form a major chord – there must be hundreds of ways to do the same thing? Yep, welcome to the infinite world of guitar!

If you're feeling ready, here are some other formulas for different types of chords to experiment with:

• Suspended 2nd (sus 2) = 1, 2, 5
• Suspended 4th (sus 4) = 1, 4, 5
(Notice with 'sus' chords you always suspend the 3rd and replace with either a 2nd or a 4th)

Try and revise this section as much as possible, so that all this new information can sink in and start making some sense!

20 QUESTIONS

This page is designed to test how much information has sunk in so far! Get yourself a blank piece of paper and write down the answers to the following 20 questions. Do not read the answers straight out of the book; you must be able to write the answers in your own words!

1. What does getting your guitar set up mean?
2. What is the action on a guitar?
3. What is considered to be good action?
4. What is a fret?
5. What is a fret board?
6. What are tuning keys and what do they do?
7. What is the claw?
8. Explain position playing.
9. What are the strings' names?
10. What is the musical alphabet?
11. How do you find notes on the guitar neck?
12. What is the note called on the 13th fret of the B string?
13. What is tablature?
14. What does a chord diagram look like?
15. What is a plectrum?
16. What do plectrums also get called?
17. What is alternate picking?
18. What is a chord progression?
19. What is a chord transition?
20. How do you build a D minor chord?

20 ANSWERS!

1. The answer can be found on page 2.
2. The answer can be found on page 2.
3. The answer can be found on page 2.
4. The answer can be found on page 3.
5. The answer can be found on page 3.
6. The answer can be found on page 3.
7. The answer can be found on page 6 and 13.
8. The answer can be found on page 9.
9. The answer can be found on page 7.
10. The answer can be found on page 7.
11. The answer can be found on page 8.
12. C
13. The answer can be found on page 10.
14. The answer can be found on page 10.
15. The answer can be found on page 5.
16. The answer can be found on page 5.
17. The answer can be found on page 13.
18. The answer can be found on page 18.
19. The answer can be found on page 19.
20. Take the 1st, flattened 3rd and 5th notes of the D major scale and arrange them into a shape that works.

PUTTING THE GROOVE INTO YOUR STRUMMING

If you have learnt how to play through the chord progressions outlined on page 24 using the chord transition ideas covered on page 25, it's time to put some 'groove' into the equation!

Groove is extremely important; it can breathe life into what you play and helps the listener connect with what you are putting across. Groove will come naturally for some of you and harder for others – regardless which of the two you are, here are a few tips to get you started!

The way I think of putting groove into strumming is to look at the guitar strings like a drum kit.

- The first three thick strings represent the **BASS** drum.

- The last three thin strings represent the **SNARE** drum.

Now think of the beat to 'We Will Rock You' by Queen.
BASS, BASS, SNARE . . . BASS, BASS, SNARE

TIME ⟶

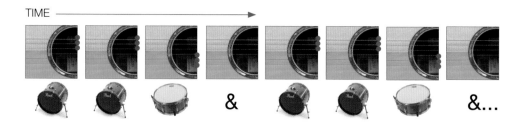

& &...

You can apply this theory to any chord progression and inject whatever feel you're capable of imagining into it! Experiment with the feel of the chord progressions you learnt on page 24.

Remember, it is very important to tap your foot when you play the guitar. It gives you a beat to be guided by and improves your general musicality; I cannot recommend tapping your foot enough!

READING CHORD PROGRESSIONS WITH COUNTING

Counting can be a great help in mastering basic chord strumming grooves. Let's look at a few common strumming grooves and break them down with counting.

Let's simplify the explanations to make reading these grooves less confusing:

D = DOWN strum   **U** = UP strum   **B** = BASS drum   **S** = SNARE drum

D/B		D/S				D/B	D/S	
1	&	**2**	&	3	**&**	**4**	&...	

Okay, now we will make the groove spread out over 8 beats and include up strums:

D/B		D/B		D/S			U/S	D/B	U/S	D/B		D/S			U/S
1	&	**2**	&	**3**	&	4	**&**	**5**	**&**	**6**	&	**7**	&	8	**&**

Always vocalise what you are playing. It's a great way to determine if you are doing it correctly or not.

Now let's get really tricky! We will practise playing a chord progression in a 3 feel (3 beats instead of 4).

C		C		C		Am		Am		Am	
D/B		D/B		D/S		D/B		D/B		D/S	
1	&	**2**	&	**3**	&	**1**	&	**2**	&	**3**	&

Em		Em		Em		G		G		G	
D/B		D/B		D/S		D/B		D/B		D/S	
1	&	**2**	&	**3**	&	**1**	&	**2**	&	**3**	&

Try and memorise these 3 strumming grooves until you feel you have mastered them. At this point you should have a good grasp of strumming down and up and knowing what to listen for when learning new songs with chord progressions.

BARRE CHORDS

Now it's time to learn the missing chords from your chord artillery – barre chords! This is what I would consider to be your first real obstacle to overcome as a beginner to the guitar.

Here is a diagram of the main 4 barre chord shapes you will come across (check out the DVD for more info about this).

E major shape barre

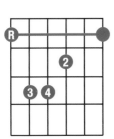 

E minor shape barre

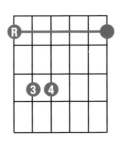 

A major shape barre

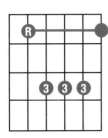 

A minor shape barre

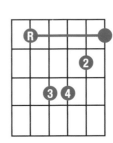 

I have labelled the 'root note'. The 'root note' is basically the note that gives the chord its name.
For example: G major is 'G' major because the root note is G.

You might notice how I have named the barre shapes: E shape, Em shape, A shape and Am shape. That is because those chords are contained within the barre chord which I have circled.

HOW TO PLAY BARRE CHORDS

Here are a few things to think about while playing barre chords. The first is to realise that the index finger doesn't have to cover every note. For E shaped barre chords, it is only the low E string, B string and high E string that need to be covered. If you can learn to angle your index finger so that the point of direct contact and strength is over those strings, then your finger can still remain relatively relaxed. Keep in mind the pressure from your thumb on the back of the neck can be used as leverage for your index finger, which is doing the barring.

 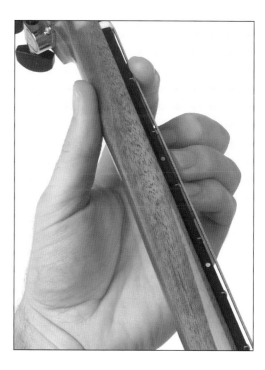

I find when I play barre chords, the point of contact on my index finger is the left hand side, with the palm facing upwards.

Another important thing to refer back too is our left hand rules and guidelines on page 18 (right hand if you are left handed). You should have a claw-like grip, with the thumb placed in the middle of the neck and (very importantly) straight – not off to the side or bent, as this will affect how your wrist and arm sits. You should not feel stress or pain whilst playing barre chords, although almost everyone does!

Looking at the diagrams, you will notice that the index finger 'bars' across the whole fret, and the remaining fingers form either an E, Em, A or Am shape. Playing what these diagrams show makes you realise the importance of good action!

HOW TO USE BARRE CHORDS

The great thing about barre chords is that they are movable shapes. There's that movable word again, and it makes life easier! You just have to move the specific barre chord shape (E, Em, A, Am) to where you want on the neck, and Bob's your uncle! So let's go through a few together.

I want to form a B major barre chord starting on the low E string:

• Using the musical alphabet, I will have to figure out where B is on the E string.
• Then, when I realise it is on the 7th fret, I will barre my index finger on the 7th fret and form the E major shape with my remaining fingers (hopefully in one pivoting movement – the band won't wait for me to make my barre chord shape!).

Now I want to play a B major barre chord starting on the low A string:

• Using the musical alphabet, I'll figure out where B is on the A string.
• When I realise it is on the 2nd fret, I'll barre my index finger on the second fret and form the A major shape with my remaining fingers.

Notice any connections? E shape barre chords are for the E string (major and minor). A shape barre chords are for the A string (major and minor).

Alternatively, if you make a barre chord on the neck and want to know what it is called:

• Ascertain whether it is major or minor by the shape (E, Em, A, Am).
• Find the root note (first note you play).
• Use your string name and musical alphabet knowledge to figure out the name of the root note.
• Voila! That's your barre chord!

MOVING ON

If you have practised and learnt everything from the previous pages, you've done extremely well. Congratulations! Now it's time to move on and discover some more complicated techniques, chords and theories. Make sure you revise often and vocalise what you have learnt while you practise it. It might make you feel crazy but I find if you cannot explain what you are doing, you don't really know, do you?

FINGER STYLE PLAYING

I feel it is vital to be adept at finger style and plectrum playing to be a good all-round guitarist. In this chapter we will go through using all of your fingers, some finger style patterns and playing through chord progressions.

I find there are two main finger style positions that I use, the first one more so than the other. Here it is:

- The thumb controls the E, A and D strings whilst the index, 2nd and 3rd fingers control the G, B and E strings.

Note: In the second main position, the thumb controls the E and A strings whilst the index, 2nd, 3rd and 4th fingers control the D, G, B, E string.

Your thumb should be in front of your other fingers and your hand should stay relatively still. I find whilst I'm using the first finger style, I tend to anchor my little finger to the guitar. Doing this ensures that your hand remains still.

FINGER STYLE PATTERNS

Here are 8 different finger style patterns using the chord progressions learnt on page 24. Notice how the tab is more for the right hand, as the chords are indicated above the tab which the left hand plays. This type of tab will generally not deviate from the confines of the specific chords written above.

- The **small numbers** indicate which fingers to use on the RIGHT HAND.
  T indicates thumb.

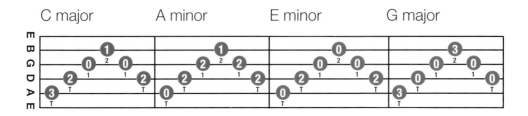

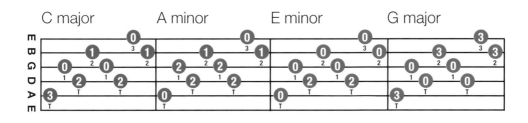

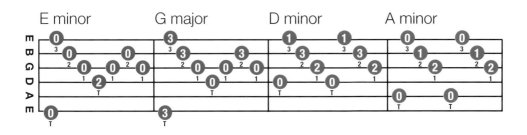

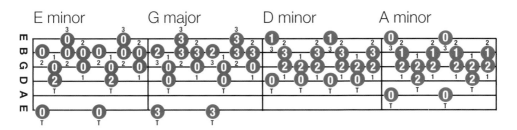

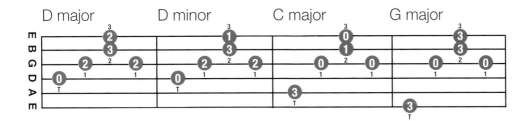

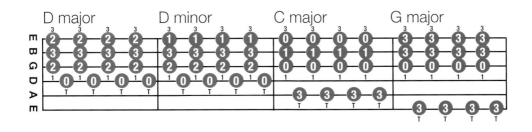

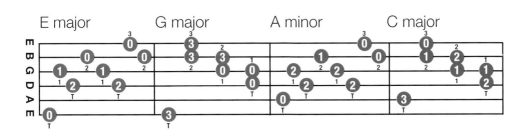

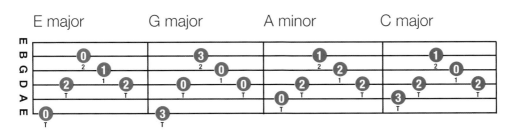

ADVANCED CHORDS

The next two pages teach four new chords which I believe are important to have in your chord 'vocabulary'. These chords have been left towards the end of the book because some shapes have open strings and other shapes are barred so it may appear a little inconsistent if you are like me and like things all neat and tidy! Aim to learn as many as you can and really take a good look at the shapes.

- Minor 7 (min7) • Dominant 7 (dom7) • Suspended 2nd (sus2) • Suspended 4th (sus4)

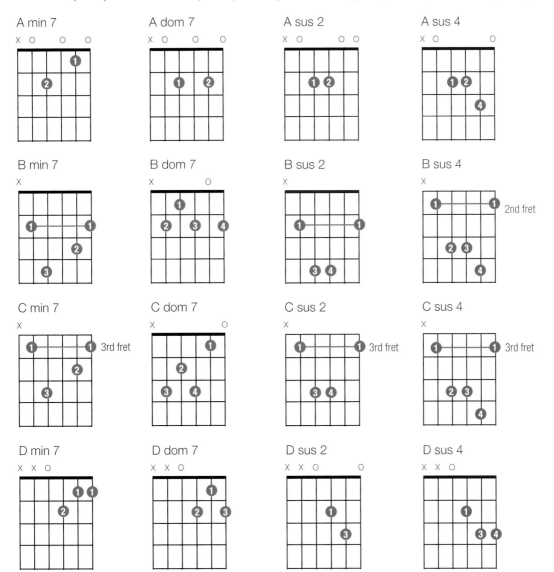

ADVANCED CHORDS

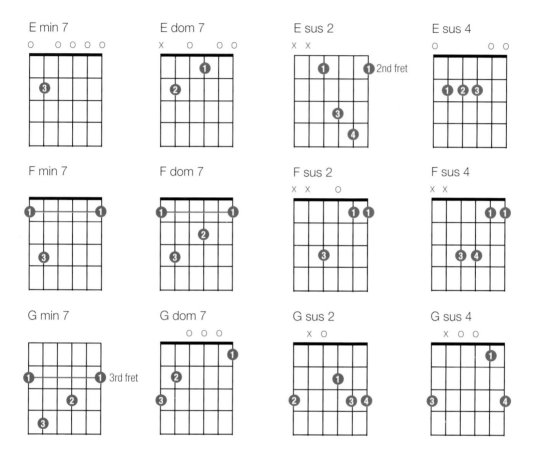

E min 7   E dom 7   E sus 2   E sus 4

F min 7   F dom 7   F sus 2   F sus 4

G min 7   G dom 7   G sus 2   G sus 4

On the last two pages I have written out the min7, dom7, sus2 and sus4 shapes in alphabetical order, featuring the basic shapes whenever possible. Just remember that some of the shapes are barre shapes, because there are no commonly used basic shapes for that particular chord.

ADVANCED CHORDS

On this page I will include just the movable barre shapes for the min7, dom7 and sus2 chords.

Min 7 (E Min 7 shape)

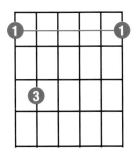

Dom 7 (E Dom 7 shape)

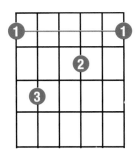

Min 7 (A Min 7 shape)

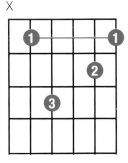

Dom 7 (A Dom 7 shape)

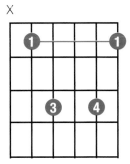

Sus 2 (A Sus 2 shape)

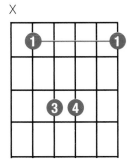

As you will notice with barre chords, the most commonly used shapes are either E or A shape based, as we discussed on page 34. For the record, you can actually turn all the basic chord shapes into barre shapes by following the same process as mentioned on page 34, but using alternate chords to the E and A shapes outlined. As you may have figured out, playing chords can be as in-depth or as simple as you want it to be!

CHORD FINDER

Here are some handy chord shapes to have at your disposal.

To find A# / Bb, C# / Db, D# / Eb, F# / Gb, G# / Ab chord shapes, simply locate the appropriate chord types marked 'movable' and move them to where you want! Remember, the first note is the 'root' note (note that gives the chord its name).

A

A maj
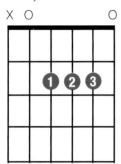

A 7
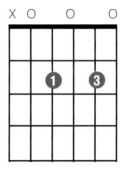

A min
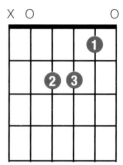

A min 7
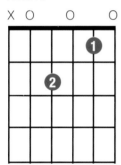

A maj 7
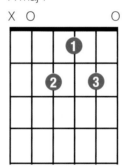

A maj 7 b5
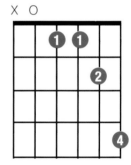

A sus 2
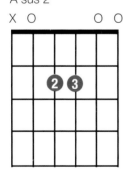

A sus 4
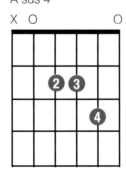

A7 sus 4
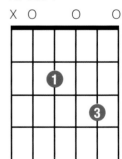

A 6
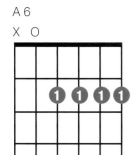

A min 6
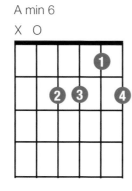

A 9
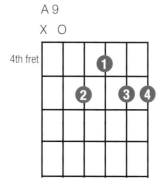

A min 9
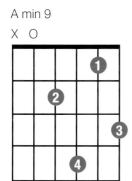

A add 9
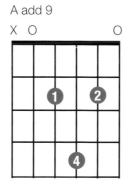

A aug   MOVABLE
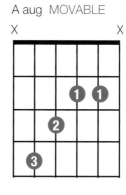

A dim
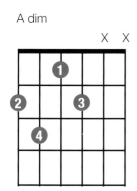

A 11
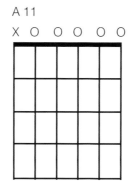

A 13
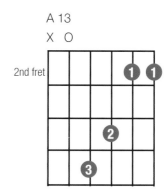

B

B maj MOVABLE
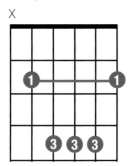

B 7
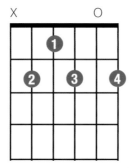

B min MOVABLE
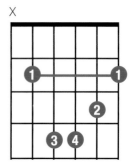

B min 7 MOVABLE
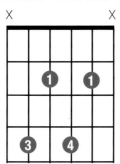

B maj 7 MOVABLE
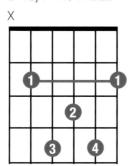

B maj 7 b5 MOVABLE
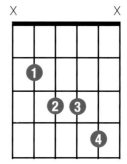

B sus 2 MOVABLE
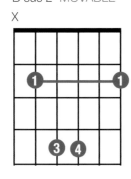

B sus 4 MOVABLE
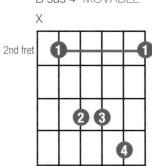

B 7 sus 4
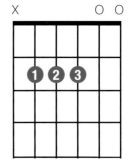

B 6
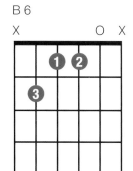

B min 6
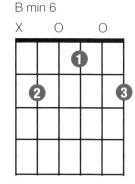

B 9 MOVABLE
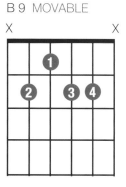

B min 9
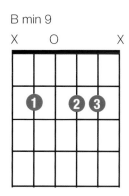

B add 9 MOVABLE
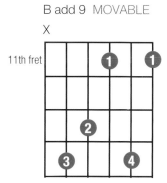

B aug
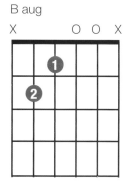

B dim
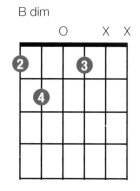

B 11 MOVABLE
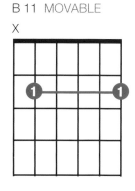

B 13 MOVABLE
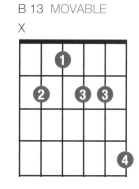

C

C maj
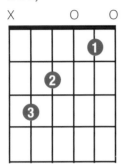

C 7
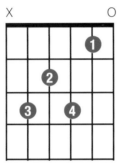

C min
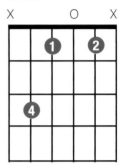

C min 7 MOVABLE
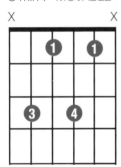

C maj 7
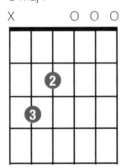

C maj 7 b5 MOVABLE
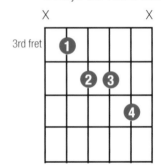

C sus 2 MOVABLE
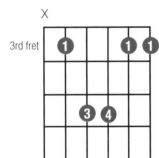

C sus 4
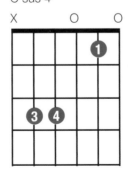

C 7 sus 4 MOVABLE
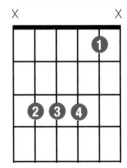

C 6 MOVABLE

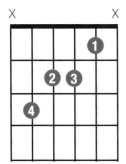

C min 6 MOVABLE

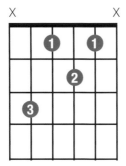

C 9 MOVABLE

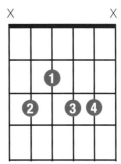

C min 9 MOVABLE

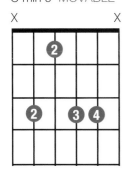

C add 9

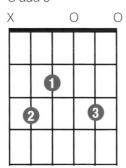

C aug MOVABLE

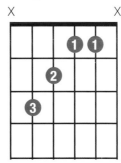

C dim MOVABLE

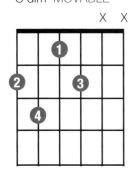

C 11 MOVABLE

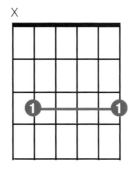

C 13 MOVABLE

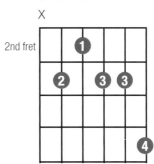

D

D maj
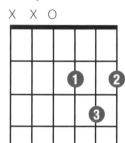

D 7
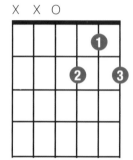

D min
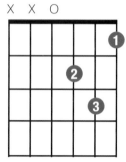

D min 7
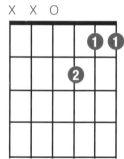

D maj 7
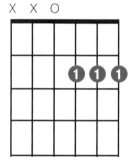

D maj 7 b5
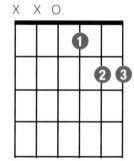

D sus 2
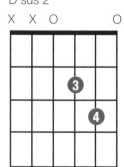

D sus 4
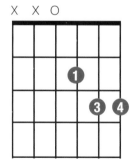

D 7 sus 4
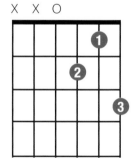

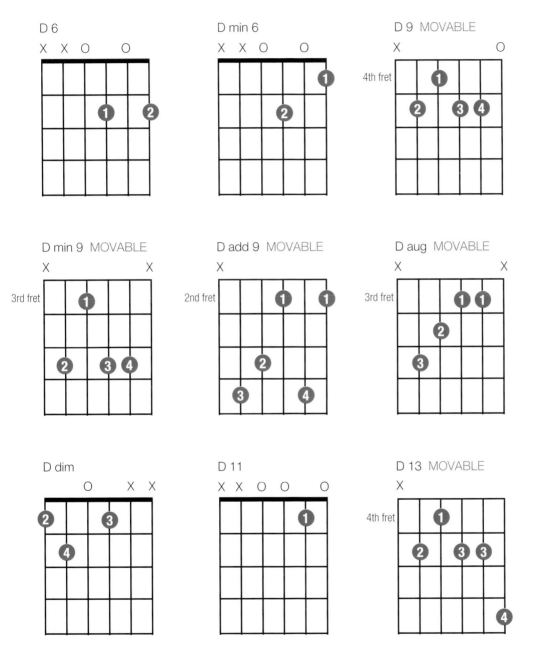

E

E maj
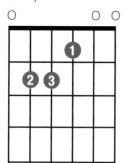

E 7
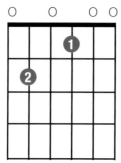

E min
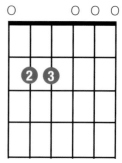

E min 7
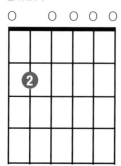

E maj 7
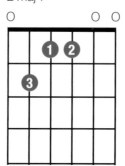

E maj 7 b5 MOVABLE
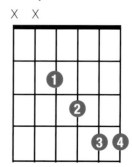

E sus 2 MOVABLE
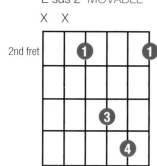

E sus 4
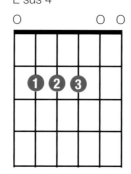

E 7 sus 4
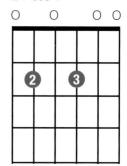

E 6

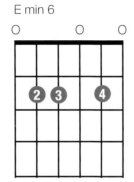

E min 6

E 9

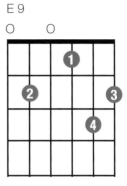

E min 9

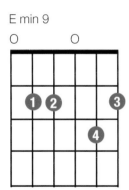

E add 9

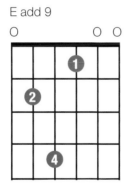

E aug

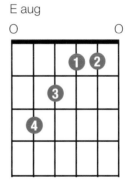

E dim MOVABLE

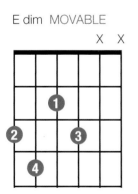

E 11

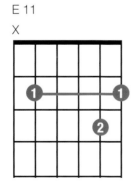

E 13

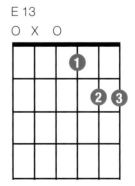

F

F maj MOVABLE

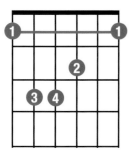

F 7 MOVABLE

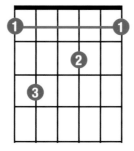

F min MOVABLE

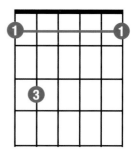

F min 7 MOVABLE

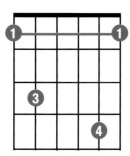

F maj 7

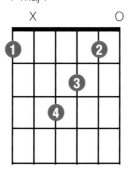

F maj 7 b5

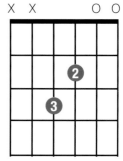

F sus 2 MOVABLE

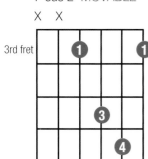

F sus 4 MOVABLE

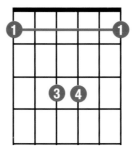

F 7 sus 4 MOVABLE

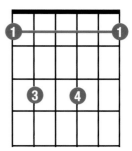

F 6 MOVABLE

X

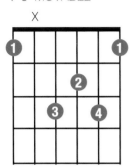

F min 6 MOVABLE

X

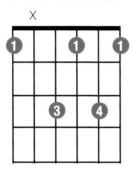

F 9

O   O

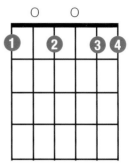

F min 9 MOVABLE

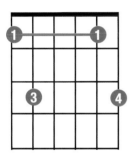

F add 9 MOVABLE

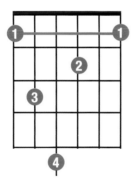

F aug MOVABLE

X   X

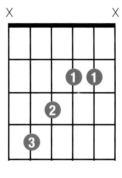

F dim

O   X X

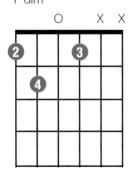

F 11 MOVABLE

X X

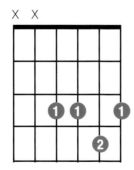

F 13 MOVABLE

X

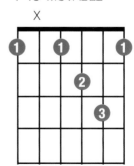

G

G maj

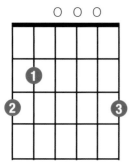

G 7

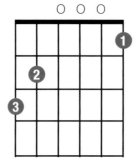

G min MOVABLE

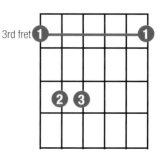

G min 7 MOVABLE

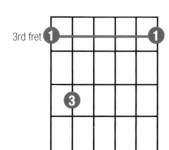

G maj 7 MOVABLE

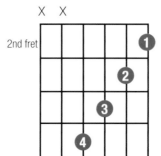

G maj 7 b5 MOVABLE

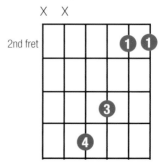

G sus 2

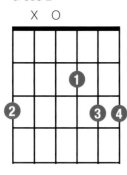

G sus 4

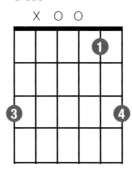

G 7 sus 4

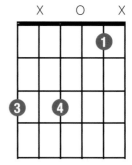

G 6

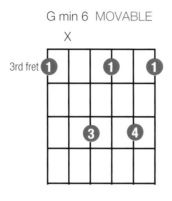

G min 6 MOVABLE

G 9 MOVABLE

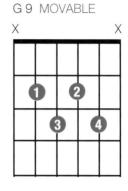

G min 9 MOVABLE

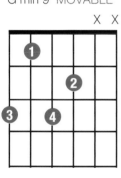

G add 9 MOVABLE

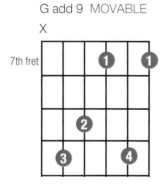

G aug

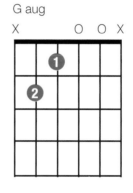

G dim MOVABLE

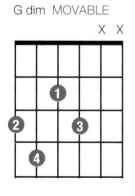

G 11 MOVABLE

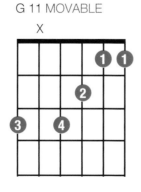

G 13

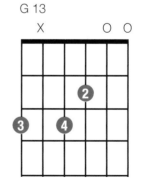

FREQUENTLY ASKED QUESTIONS

• When should I change my guitar strings?

I think it's a good idea to change your strings as often as possible. Don't leave it until your strings go black and feel like barbed wire before you change them. I actually change my strings before every gig.

• How long until I get calluses on my fingertips?

That depends on how much you play. If you play a lot, it takes less time. In general, I believe it usually takes a few months of solid playing to harden the tips of your fingers properly. So get cracking!

• Can a guitar ever be perfectly in tune?

Yes. If you have a good quality guitar and it has been set up properly, you should be able to achieve a perfectly tuned guitar. On the flip side, if you want to get scientific, in tune is probably never completely attainable down to the most minute level, but to the human ear, it will sound in tune!

• How do I play faster?

In my opinion, playing fast is more about perfecting slow playing, then gradually increasing speed. There are a few explanations about that philosophy. Firstly, 'perfection' means perfect technique from both hands with robot-like precision. Secondly, gradually increasing speed may be done over the course of many months, not one hour. People who can play guitar at the speed of light are just the same as you, only they have trained their fingers and brain to execute their playing with great precision. It is just like learning how to walk using motor skills – you start out wobbly and end up doing it with ease, but it takes a lot of time and dedication to practice.

• How do you write songs?

The short answer is, any way you like!

I always relate music to cooking – if you know how to cook; you know that certain spices and ingredients complement each other. If you don't know how to cook, you may end up stumbling on an amazing creation, or make something that the snails wouldn't eat. My advice is to start listening and trying to analyse songs that you love and find out why you love them. Why does that chord work so well with that other chord? Why does that melody sound so great over that chord? To get anywhere in music, I think you have to always ask a lot of questions and try and dissect the things that appeal to you.

• Why does my guitar always go out of tune?

There is a lot of different ways your guitar can go out of tune. Exposing your guitar to a change in climate is probably one of the most common reasons. Every time you take it outside, you can affect the tuning. If your guitar is in a soft case and not a hard case, the bag can touch the tuning keys and put it out of tune. Obviously if you bump the tuning keys or have poor quality tuning keys that move or are loose, it can affect the tuning. If you change the gauge (thickness) of strings without having it set up for that gauge, you can put stress on the neck, which will make the guitar go out of tune.

• Does guitar get harder from the level I am at now?

Guitar can be as complicated as you want. You could always learn more, play more, play better. Even the greatest guitarists on earth have challenges – they just differ as you progress.

• How long does it take to be as good as the rock stars?

You would be surprised how many professional guitarists aren't that good! It's more about interpretation and originality in some cases, and in some cases neither. To answer your question, it all depends on which rock stars you are referring to! I would say if you learnt from a good teacher and practised rigorously, you could be playing like some of today's rock stars in a couple of years.

CONCLUSION

To benefit from this book, I recommend you review all the material as often as you can. Make sure you fully understand everything that has been discussed before you move on to other subjects.

The most important things to remember are the two 'Ps'; patience and practice. Be patient enough to slow things down and run them over and over, refining your technique with the tips outlined in this book and practise daily.

You will not progress if you don't practise. I cannot stress enough the importance of daily practice and a regimented, disciplined approach to doing so. Practise all of the priority topics before you mess around. Allocate a few minutes each day to focus purely on your technique. Critique your own playing – could you do that better? Is your technique as good as it could be? Does that sound as good as when your teacher plays it? 15 minutes practice Monday to Sunday is better than no practice during the week and eight hours on the weekend.

Consolidate your knowledge. I teach a lot of students things that they don't realise they already know, simply because they haven't 'joined the dots'. For example, if I can play a G major chord, I also know that the root note is a G note. Therefore, I know where the G note is on the neck. Using the musical alphabet, I can easily find F# or G# or any surrounding notes from that G note.

Make sure you think about everything you have learnt and everything you know, and try and 'join the dots'. Try and apply the knowledge you have to your playing.

Listen to great guitar players. Listen to the guitar in songs that you like. Always try and define what you like about them and what you don't like. Talk to musicians. Use the internet. Buy videos and books to further your understanding of guitar. Get a good teacher. Try a few different teachers. Play with other guitar players, even if they are beginners. Teach other people what you know, because verbalising and teaching is a great way to reinforce what you yourself have learnt.

In conclusion, I hope that you have understood my explanations and learnt a lot more than you knew before reading this book!

Keep playing!

Steve MacKay

ABOUT THE AUTHOR

Steve MacKay is an internationally recognised guitarist and professional guitar teacher. He started playing guitar at age 8 and now regularly plays, writes and produces music with some of the biggest names in the music industry.

Steve has accompanied Delta Goodrem on her promotional tours around North America and Europe, sometimes playing in front of crowds of over 10,000 people.

He has performed on television programs such as *Top of the Pops* and *The MTV Music Awards* in Australia, New Zealand, the UK, Germany, the Netherlands and Canada with artists such as Delta Goodrem, Kelly Clarkson and Brian McFadden.

Steve has worked with international producers and songwriters Billy Mann (Jessica Simpson, Pink, Hall and Oates, Michael Bolton, Sting, Art Garfunkel) and Eliot Kennedy and Gary Barlow (Celine Dion, Spice Girls, Bryan Adams, Atomic Kitten). He has written, produced and played on songs for Christine Anu, Delta Goodrem, Brian McFadden and Australian music legend Brian Cadd, and has recorded sessions for television and film programs such as the *Mighty Morphin' Power Rangers* (Disney) and *The Secret Life of Us*.

Steve would like to say...

THANK YOU to the two most influential guitar teachers I have had: Tony Calabro and Samantha Rainy.